PRIMATES
LEMURS, MONKEYS, AND YOU

BY IAN TATTERSALL

Beyond Museum Walls
The Millbrook Press
Brookfield, Connecticut

Cover photograph: Courtesy of Tom McHugh

Photographs courtesy and © Jay H. Matternes: pp. 19, 23, 34, 51; Ian Tattersall:
pp. 24, 45 (top), 64; David Haring: pp. 26 (both), 27, 29 (all); Elwyn Simons:
p. 33; Photo Researchers: pp. 37 (Tom McHugh), 39 (Stephen Dalton), 40
(Andrew L. Young), 46 (Mark D. Phillips); Robert Sussman: pp. 43 (both), 45
(bottom); Anthro-Photo: pp. 54 (Robert Bailey), 57 (Irv DeVore), 59 (A. H.
Harcourt), 61 (James Moore). Illustrations on pp. 10 and 15 © Diana Salles.

Library of Congress Cataloging-in-Publication Data
Tattersall, Ian.
Primates: lemurs, monkeys, and you / by Ian Tattersall.
p.   cm. — (Beyond museum walls)
Includes bibliographical references (p.   ) and index.
SUMMARY: Presents the primate family, including lower primates such as
lemurs and lorises and higher primates such as monkeys and apes, with emphasis
on how its members evolved and similarities and differences among them.
ISBN 1-56294-520-3 (lib. bdg.)
1. Human evolution—Juvenile literature.   2. Primates—Evolution—
Juvenile literature.   I. Title.   II. Series.
GN281.T37   1995   573.2—dc20   94-15072   CIP

Published by The Millbrook Press
2 Old New Milford Road, Brookfield, Connecticut 06804
Series editor: Margaret Cooper

CONTENTS

PRIMATES

INTRODUCTION

Imagine that you are at a party, with all of your relatives there, too. But who are these relatives? This is a strange assortment of guests. Over there in a dark corner is a tiny creature from Madagascar called a mouse lemur. He's talking to a saucer-eyed night monkey from South America, who also prefers the gloom. In the center of the room, where it's brighter, a huge gorilla is munching a stick of celery and chatting with a lithe, long-legged patas monkey. Both are from Africa, but they don't get to see each other much because one lives in tropical forest and the other on the fringes of the Sahara Desert.

The guy with the big nose is a proboscis monkey from Borneo, and he's deep in conversation with an elegant colobus monkey from Africa, who's wearing a spectacular coat of long, luxuriant black and white fur. That silvery blur who just whizzed across the room in a single leap is a sifaka from Madagascar; he was anxious to have a word with his distant cousin the gibbon, from Malaysia, whom he saw hanging idly from the chandelier near the entrance. Worryingly, though, all of the guests are glancing nervously from time to time at you, standing in the doorway.

What kind of party is this? It's a primates' party, and all the guests are primates, members of the same major group of animals to which we belong. This book is about the primates: what they are, how they began, how they evolved, and how they live. And we'll start right at the beginning, with a look at where primates fit into nature as a whole.

CHAPTER ONE

HUMANS IN THE LIVING WORLD

Earth is home to many millions of different kinds of living things. All of them are related, by descent from a very, very ancient ancestor that lived more than three and a half billion years ago. So even though you and I may appear to differ enormously from, say, a bamboo or a mushroom or a cockroach, we all have certain things in common that we have inherited from that remote ancestor.

Just as each of us has our own family tree, showing our descent from our great-grandparents, grandparents, and parents, this long history of ancestry allows us to think of the great diversity of life as forming a sort of evolutionary tree, or bush. The ancient ancestor of us all lies right at the root, while the ancestor of each major group of living things sits at the base of each large branch. Each branch then divides and divides again, until we reach the tiny terminal twigs that represent all the world's living species, among them our own, *Homo sapiens*.

Like most living species, we have a body that is made up of many cells, the tiny structures that combine to form our tissues and organs. However, our most ancient ancestor consisted of only a single cell, so it's not surprising that the inheritance that all living things share from that most ancient common ancestor is hidden deep within each of our cells. This

inheritance consists of tiny *nucleic acids* that can be seen only with the most powerful of microscopes. It is these nucleic acids, in the form of *genes*, that allow us to pass our characteristics from one generation to the next.

All living things thus possess nucleic acids. But once we get past this common bond with every other living thing, we find that life comes in a vast variety of different forms. These range from microscopic bacteria and worms to rats and giant whales, not to mention seaweed, mosses, and maple trees. This may look like a bewildering diversity, but it is not random. It is organized into a large number of groups whose members have traits in common—and within the large groups we can easily see smaller groups that have even more in common.

For example, we belong to a major group called Vertebrata. These are the animals with backbones, and they include fish and reptiles and birds as well as us and our furry, warm-blooded mammal relatives. But although when you eat a fish it's easy to see that it has a head and a backbone as we do, it's also obvious that a fish has no arms or legs. Only *vertebrates* that live on the land have such limbs. They have arms and legs because the first land-dwelling vertebrate had them, and passed them along to its descendants.

But by now, some 350 million years later, those land-dwellers have become a pretty varied group. Some have taken to the air; these are the birds, which are clothed in feathers and whose forelimbs have become

Mammals from all over the world show amazing variety: A gopher rests in its burrow; just above it are a warthog, a red panda, and a jackrabbit. A scale-covered pangolin (a member of the anteater family that lives in Asia and Africa) has started up the tree; a flying fox (a type of bat) hangs from one tree branch, and two monkeys (golden lion tamarins) rest on another. Below them are a rhinoceros, two lions chasing a sable antelope, an elephant, a camel, and a kangaroo. In the background are elephant seals, a killer whale, and a mountain goat.

transformed into wings. Others are scaly; these are the reptiles. And yet others are furry; these are mammals, ourselves among them.

But even mammals come in a huge number of varieties, from giant whales and elephants to tiny shrews and mice. Some mammals live in deserts, others in jungles. Some live in the steamy tropics, others in the snow-covered wastes of the Arctic. Some swim, some run, some burrow, some glide or even fly. Some eat grasses; others eat fruit or flowers or the leaves of trees or other animals. Some are active during the day, others at night or around the clock. Some live in giant herds, some in family groups, and some live solitary lives. Some depend on their noses to find food, others on their eyes. Some have hoofs, some have claws, some have grasping hands. In other words, mammals have managed to occupy just about every *habitat* possible, and to exploit these different habitats in almost every possible way.

Where do we humans fit among this great variety of mammals? Well, scientists have divided the mammals into a number of major groups called orders. The order Rodentia, for example, contains the gnawing mammals: rats, mice, squirrels, and all the many other forms that have ever-growing front teeth that allow them to gnaw their way through tough substances. The order Artiodactyla contains the cloven-hoofed mammals and their relatives, including deer, antelope, and camels. The order to which we belong is called Primates (pronounced pry-MAY-tees when used as a proper noun, with the first letter capitalized), and it is the primates (pronounced PRY-mates when a common noun) that are the subject of this book. Besides ourselves, the order Primates contains the lorises, bushbabies, lemurs, tarsiers, monkeys, and apes.

CHAPTER TWO

WHAT ARE PRIMATES?

Ever since the order Primates was named more than two centuries ago, scientists have been arguing over how to define that order. The problem is that all primates living today are descended from an ancestor that lived more than 65 million years ago. And during those 65 million years of *evolution* there has been plenty of time for the many descendants of that ancestor to change so much that tracing their connection with the ancestor is tricky. There are well over 200 species of primates living today in Africa, Asia, and Central and South America, and they are a varied lot indeed. But not one of them resembles the ancient common ancestor at all closely, and they differ enormously among themselves. So finding even one special feature that all primates share today, let alone with their earlier ancestors, is a tough job indeed.

One clever way of getting around the problem of definition has been to describe primates in terms of a set of evolutionary "trends" that have generally marked the evolution of this group. Here are some of them.

Primates tend to retain a rather unspecialized body form. In other words, they have many of the features of early mammals that other kinds of mammals have lost as they adapted to particular ways of life. For example, primates have the original five-fingered hand that has been lost by mammals like sheep and horses, which evolved hoofs useful for moving quickly over hard ground. Primates also have a collarbone, which has disappeared during the evolution of many mammal groups.

The fingers of primate hands tend to move freely; and the thumb, which "faces" the other fingers, permits strong grasping. Claws have been lost from the ends of the fingers and toes. Instead, they are tipped by flat nails, which provide a backing for sensitive pads. These pads give us our exquisite sense of touch.

The faces of primates have tended to become shorter from front to back, especially as the sense of smell has become less acute. At the same time, the eyes have moved toward the front of the head so that the fields of vision of each eye overlap. Many mammals, by contrast, have eyes that are almost on opposite sides of the head. By putting together the similar views from each eye, our brains can provide us with three-dimensional vision that gives a sense of depth. And those brains themselves have shown a definite tendency toward becoming bigger and more complex.

Another primate trend is the development of better means of nourishing new individuals as they develop within the mother before birth. Periods of development before birth tend to lengthen, too. A mouse fetus develops for only three or four weeks before the new mouse is born, whereas a gorilla fetus needs nine months. At the same time, primates tend to live longer than most other mammals. And they are built so that it is relatively easy for them to walk on two legs if they have to.

Many mammal groups show one or more of these tendencies. But only primates show all of them, and some do so to a greater degree than others. We should also not forget that this list of trends was selected by human beings, and that humans show nearly all of them in their most extreme forms.

Human hands, for example, can manipulate objects with the finest precision. Another example is how we depend on our sense of vision, with

Members of the primate family have certain traits in common. But the different types developed over millions of years in ways that suited various habitats and ways of life.

smell playing a minor role in exploring the world around us. The size of our face is thus greatly reduced, but we have a much-expanded braincase to contain the most complex brain we know of in the living world. We spend a very long time developing inside our mothers before birth, and once we are born we enjoy the longest life expectancy of any primate.

As mentioned above, tendencies such as larger brain size and increasing importance of vision show to different degrees in different primates living now. So sometimes we talk about "lower" and "higher" primates, as if there were a ladder of evolution, with lemurs at the bottom, monkeys and apes next, and ourselves at the top. These terms are very misleading. Every primate species living today has an evolutionary history just as long as our own. All have adapted over millions of years to their own particular habitats and ways of life. Lemurs may look more "primitive" than we are. But it's just not correct to see any other primates as "living ancestors." They don't represent steps on a ladder that leads to ourselves. They are individual species with their own long histories, adaptations, and unique places in nature.

How did this great variety of primates come about? To find out, we have to look at the *fossil* record, which tells us about the life of the past.

CHAPTER THREE

BACK TO THE BEGINNING

The evolutionary history of the primates, as of all other living things, is recorded by fossils. Primate fossils almost always represent teeth and bones, the hard parts of the body that are most likely to resist decay and to be preserved in newly forming rocks.

Teeth and bones tell us a lot. For example, by comparing different teeth and bones we can discover which other animals each fossil species was most closely related to, and thus fix its place in nature. They also tell us something about how the animal lived. For example, the shape of a fossil mammal's teeth can tell us about the kinds of things it ate, while the shape of its bones can provide information about how it moved around. Very often the fossils we find are just broken bits and pieces rather than complete skulls and skeletons. Even then, there's quite a lot we're usually able to discover from them.

The fossils themselves don't tell the whole story, however. The rocks in which they're found can be informative, too. They tell us, for example, how long ago the fossil animals in them lived. They can also tell us about the conditions in which those animals lived—what the climate was like, for instance, and whether the area was sea, swamp, or mountains. And fossils of different animals can tell something about each other, too. Thus, if you are particularly interested in a fossil that is found together with fossils of other animals that are adapted to an open-country environment, you can be pretty sure that your fossil animal of interest also lived in open country.

The earliest fossils that may be those of primates are a handful of tiny teeth from rocks in the western United States that date from the very end of the Age of Dinosaurs, about 65 million years ago. Until that time the mammals were a not very diverse group of rather nondescript, small-bodied species that were probably active at night. But the disappearance of the dinosaurs at around that time opened up new evolutionary horizons for the mammals—and primates were among the first mammals to grab the new opportunities. During the Paleocene epoch (about 65 to 58 million years ago), the opening period of the Age of Mammals, primates flourished widely in Eurasia and North America—and probably in Africa, too, though we have no fossil record there to go by.

These early primates were not like any of the primates that we know today. Compared to any modern primates, they had very small brains, and their big faces suggest that they depended a lot on the sense of smell in exploring their environment. Their eyes faced quite a bit sideways, and they probably didn't have very good depth perception. They were quite heavily built, and did not have grasping hands; instead, their fingers and toes were tipped with claws. Altogether, they were rather squirrellike. They even had very large incisor teeth at the front of their mouths, though these teeth didn't grow constantly, as those of squirrels do.

The best-known of these primates is the genus *Plesiadapis*, whose fossils are found on both sides of what was then a much narrower Atlantic Ocean. What made *Plesiadapis* and its relatives primatelike was their teeth. These had become rather flattened and bulbous, in contrast to the high, pointy teeth, ideal for puncturing insect "shells," that had been typical of earlier mammals. It seems likely that the first primates were moving away

Plesiadapis, one of the earliest primates, was more like a squirrel than like any primate of today.

from a diet of insects toward a more varied one that included a lot of fruit. Fruits were becoming increasingly available in the forests as the flowering plants spread after their origin during the Age of Dinosaurs.

It's quite certain that *Plesiadapis* and the other early primates lived in a forest setting, but it's not so clear that they spent all or even most of their time in the trees. Some of them at least may have spent a good part of their lives on the forest floor, perhaps eating ripe fruit that had fallen from the trees as well as snuffling around in the leaf litter for any other edibles they might find. Actually, the early primates form a pretty *diverse* group, and it's likely that members of this group adopted quite a number of different lifeways as they expanded over time into a wide range of places and habitats. Studies of fossil teeth suggest, for example, that eventually members of this group came to specialize on many different foods, such as gums, sap, leaves, fruit, and so forth. And in contrast to the mammals of the Age of Dinosaurs, which were all pretty certainly active only at night, it's possible that some of the earliest primates were active during the day.

Some scientists have recently begun to suggest that *Plesiadapis* and its relatives may not have been "true" primates, but instead were members of a wider group that contained ancestral bats, colugos ("flying lemurs"), and tree shrews as well. Whatever the case, however, it's pretty certain that we can look upon these mammals as reasonably good "models" of what our earliest ancestors were like. So it's a pity that they are so unlike any primates today that we don't have much basis for guessing about their social behavior.

CHAPTER FOUR

"TRUE" PRIMATES APPEAR

A species that lived maybe 60 million years ago was the first of the "modern" primates in the sense that it resembled primates alive today. While it's not particularly useful or accurate to think of various primates as occupying points on a scale from "more primitive" to "more advanced," it's nonetheless true in a general sense that today's "lower" primates resemble that ancient common ancestor more closely than the "higher" primates do.

Accordingly, modern primates are classified into two major groups or suborders. Informally, we can think of these as the lower and higher primates; more formally, they are often known as *prosimians* and *anthropoids*. Prosimians alive now include the lemurs of Madagascar, a large island off the east coast of Africa, plus the lorises and bushbabies of Africa and Asia and the Asian tarsiers. The anthropoids include the monkeys of the Old and New Worlds, the lesser and greater apes, and humans.

EARLY PROSIMIANS ▪ The first of the modern primates to appear on the scene were the prosimians. They flourished during the Eocene epoch, which lasted from about 58 to 35 million years ago. As we've seen, they broadly resembled today's lemurs and lorises. They had grasping hands and feet, with the thumbs and big toes separated from the other fingers and toes. Compared to body size, the early prosimians had bigger brains than the earlier primates had. And their faces were somewhat smaller, suggesting that the sense of smell was less important. Along with this, the eyes were moved forward on the face, to give more overlapping fields of vision and better depth perception. A bony strut on the side stabilized the eye. This meant that the eye sockets were completely encircled (though not encased) by bone—something that was lacking in the Paleocene ancestors. However, it's unlikely that they had color vision, even though it's almost certain that many of them were active during the day.

The Eocene primates are generally divided into two major groups. One of these groups is most often compared to the present-day lemurs of Madagascar. It consisted mostly of quite large-bodied (cat-sized) and probably day-active species, for example those of *Notharctus*. The other major group is usually thought to be related to the tarsier of Southeast Asia. It consisted of smaller species, most of which appear to have been active at night.

As we will see, today's prosimians show a wide range of diets and social groupings, and it seems quite likely that this range of behavior was also typical of the Eocene primates. During the Eocene, world climate was a good bit warmer than it is today, so that the primates—tropical animals then, as now—lived in a wider variety of places than their modern descendants. For example, they flourished in the forests of North America and Europe, regions in which primates other than humans are unknown today.

Since the closest comparable animals to the Eocene primates are some of the prosimians living now, let's look briefly at these modern primates. The best place to start is Madagascar, since this huge island off the East African coast is home to most of today's prosimians, more than thirty species of them. Madagascar's prosimians are known as lemurs, and among them are the only living prosimians that are active in the daytime.

This mother and baby *Notharctus* belonged to a group of early primates that were much like present-day lemurs.

A baby ring-tailed lemur clings tightly to its mother.

LEMURS ▪ There are several families of lemurs. The most familiar are the "true" lemurs. Among several species of these is the ring-tailed lemur, the only living prosimian that spends a considerable amount of time on the ground. The true lemurs walk, run, climb, and leap using all four legs. Their diets vary, but all include leaves and fruit. They live in several different kinds of groups. There are "families" that include an adult male and female with their young offspring, small groups with at most two or three adults of each sex, and larger troops of almost thirty, with several adult males and females plus offspring. Some true lemurs are active only at night, at least during certain seasons of the year. Others are active on and off throughout the 24-hour daily cycle. Still others are active mostly during the day.

All lemurs have a range of calls that they use for communication with group members and neighboring groups. Like other lemurs, true lemurs also "mark" their territories, using scents produced by specialized glands. They rub these glands on branches (and sometimes on each other), leaving an odor which can linger for quite a long time. These odors are like "calling cards," leaving information for other animals that may come along later.

Another group of lemurs contains the sifakas. They have very long legs which they use to jump surprising distances between tree trunks—sometimes 30 feet (9 meters) or more. Sifakas are extraordinarily athletic and graceful, and when they are on the ground they bounce along on their hind limbs in a very typical way. Maybe you've seen television films of them doing this; if you have, you'll find it hard to forget! Among this group are the indris, or babakotos, the largest of the living lemurs, which may weigh about 15 pounds (7 kilograms).

The smallest lemur, in contrast, is the aptly named mouse lemur, which weighs only a couple of ounces. These tiny primates eat insects, fruit, and flowers. The small home ranges of several females may be overlapped by the range of a single male. The dwarf lemur family to which mouse lemurs belong includes several species. All have huge eyes, which show that they are active at night. Large eyes can make the best use of the little light available. Most of the night is spent foraging alone, but in some species males and females may come together for a while during the night's activities, and individuals (most often females) may huddle together in nests during the daytime sleeping period.

Above: Sifakas can leap amazing distances. Left: The tiny mouse lemur is active at night.

**The aye-aye uses its long, thin middle finger
to probe for insect grubs in dead wood.**

The oddest of all the lemurs are the aye-ayes. These cat-sized creatures are active only at night and have strange faces dominated by enormous gnawing front teeth. They use these teeth for a variety of tasks, and
most especially for obtaining insects from beneath the bark of trees or the
inside of hard nuts. With their huge ears they can listen for insect larvae
tunneling inside dead tree branches. When they hear one, they tear the
branch apart with their strong front teeth, then probe with their extraordinary long, slender middle fingers until the grub is speared.

Until people arrived in Madagascar less than 2,000 years ago, many other lemur species lived there as well. Almost all of them were a lot bigger than the lemurs that are still there; one was bigger than a gorilla! They also had a remarkable variety of lifestyles, though all were probably active during the day. One was completely adapted for life on the ground, and another hung in the trees rather like a sloth! But these bigger forms were easier targets for human hunters than the smaller ones. They also were more severely affected when people burned and cleared their forest habitat. In a short time they became extinct as the result of the human activities that continue to threaten nonhuman primates around the world.

OTHER PROSIMIANS ▪ Outside Madagascar, prosimian primates today are all *nocturnal*, probably as a means of surviving alongside the day-active monkeys. It seems likely that all are more closely related to the dwarf lemurs than to the other prosimians.

There are three families of these primates. The first contains the quite small lorises of Asia and pottos of Africa, which climb carefully in the trees and rarely if ever leap. They are particularly good at preying on insects; they creep softly up on an insect and grab it before it can jump or fly to safety.

The second family contains the bushbabies of Africa, which are remarkable leapers. The smallest of them are the size of the tiny mouse lemurs, and the largest weigh no more than a couple of pounds. Bushbabies bound between tree trunks and branches, and feed on insects, fruit, and the gums that seep from tree trunks. As with the dwarf lemurs, the home ranges of males are larger than those of females; and while males tend to compete with each other, females are much more sociable among themselves.

The third prosimian family contains just the tarsiers, tiny nocturnal primates that live on certain islands of Indonesia and the Philippines.

Top left: The bush baby can leap from tree to tree. Top right: The pygmy slow loris creeps along tree branches in search of insects. Right: This Philippine tarsier's huge eyes help it see and catch prey in the dark.

Tarsiers are a great puzzle; scientists have for long been uncertain how to classify them. Do they belong with the lemurs and lorises, or with the higher primates in the anthropoid group? Many scientists would vote for the anthropoids. But on the face of it, tarsiers look much more like prosimians, and that's how we'll view them here. With their large heads, huge eyes, and short little faces, tarsiers look like very endearing creatures. However, they are fierce *predators*, and are the only primates that feed solely on other animals: small snakes, lizards, insects, and so forth. Although tarsiers weigh not much more than a quarter of a pound (113 grams), they have very long ankles and hind limbs, which allow them to hop across gaps in the forest that are as much as 20 feet (6 meters) wide.

While tarsiers today boast only a few species restricted to a tiny area of the world, in the Eocene the animals believed to be their relatives were numerous and widespread. It has often been thought that the ancestor of today's higher primates belonged to this fossil group, though some scientists argue for a lemur ancestry. If the truth be told, however, it's almost impossible to identify any convincing ancestor for the higher primates among the fossils known from the Eocene. There are not enough fossils from this time to tell us what we need to know. But by the time we get to the next geological epoch, we find fossils that definitely are identifiable as anthropoids.

CHAPTER FIVE

"HIGHER" PRIMATES ARRIVE ON THE SCENE

The anthropoids alive today include the monkeys of Central and South America and those of Africa and Asia. They also include the gibbons (the "lesser" apes), and the great apes: chimpanzees, gorillas, and orangutans. In terms of common ancestry, people definitely belong in the great ape group, though we prefer to separate ourselves out as "humans."

Compared to the prosimians, anthropoids generally have a larger and more elaborate brain. Related to this feature is an increase in intelligence and a generally more complex kind of social life. Young anthropoids grow up more slowly than prosimians do, and in their extended growing-up period the young learn a great deal about their world and about how to relate to other members of their social group.

Anthropoids have good color vision, and the eyes are placed right at the front of the head, looking straight forward and giving excellent depth perception. Possibly this innovation was connected in some way with a change to daytime activity. Among all the anthropoids, only the night monkeys of South America are active at night, and this behavior probably developed rather recently. The eyes of anthropoids are also protected and stabilized at the back by a sheet of bone (as are those of tarsiers, but in a different way).

Along with these changes in the visual system is a further reduction of the organs of smell. For example, the "wet nose," familiar in dogs and also found in prosimians, is gone. The lesser importance of the sense of smell is reflected in the behavior of anthropoids. Among all the many different kinds, only a few South American species have scent glands and use odor in communication. The higher primates also have better hand control than the prosimians do. While prosimians usually grasp objects using the whole hand, anthropoids are able to use their fingers independently, and thus can handle things more precisely. Prosimians tend to investigate an object—a ripe fruit, say—by sniffing it, rather than exploring it with their eyes and turning it in their hands as we do. So our larger brains, increased intelligence, better vision, reduced sense of smell, and better ability to handle things all seem to fit together as part of a single package.

EARLY ANTHROPOIDS ▪ We will look more closely at the many kinds of living "higher" primates in later chapters. For the moment, we'll stay with the evolution of the earliest higher primates. We begin to find these in the fossil record at the very end of the Eocene epoch and in the Oligocene epoch (about 35 to 24 million years ago) which followed. Before we go further, though, it's important to understand that the "monkeys" of the Old and New Worlds do not form a single group. In other words, the term "monkey" is just a convenient word to use for the "higher" primates that are not apes or humans.

The New World monkeys are a separate group whose evolutionary history is distinct from that of the Old World monkeys, apes, and humans. All Old World primates are descended from a more recent common ancestor than the one they share with the New World primates.

Unfortunately, the fossil record of the earliest anthropoids is not very good. Almost all of the very early fossils that we have come from a single place in northern Africa—the Fayum Depression in Egypt. The fossil-bearing rocks there seem to date from the latest part of the Eocene and the earliest part of the Oligocene, perhaps between about 36 and 32 million years ago.

At that time, far from resembling the barren desert of today, this area was a low-lying region of tropical forest, with broad rivers running sluggishly through it as they approached the nearby ocean. Crocodiles yawned on the riverbanks, and the trees teemed with primates of many kinds. Very recently scientists have discovered fossil relatives of the lemurs and tarsiers in the Fayum, together with some peculiar fossils that are thought to be anthropoids largely because they have bone-enclosed eye sockets.

Best represented, however, are two ancient groups with the rather unpronounceable names of *parapithecids* and *propliopithecids*. The parapithecids are generally viewed as "monkeylike" from their general appearance and how we think they behaved. Scientists disagree about whether

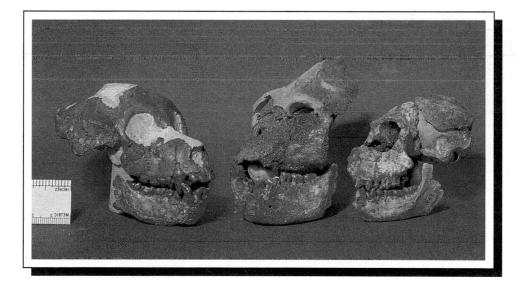

Fossilized skulls of early primates, between 36 and 32 million years old, were found in northern Africa.

Aegyptopithecus probably lived in groups
and rarely came down from the trees.

they were ancestral to one of today's monkey groups, but they probably weren't.

The second group, the propliopithecids, is the most interesting to those concerned with modern anthropoid origins. Although its significance is debated too, this family may have contained the ancestor of both the Old World and the New World higher primates. At first this might seem a bit unlikely, because Africa and South America are separated today by a vast ocean. But the continents have moved over millions of years, and back in Eocene times Africa and South America were a lot closer together. Also, North America, with its large variety of prosimians, was at that time far away to the north. So it appears likely that the ancestral South American monkeys "island-hopped" their way from Africa to South America some time late in the Eocene, when the two continents were not too far apart. Unfortunately, the fossil record in South America is pretty limited. Mainly what it tells us is that today's families of South American monkeys tend to go back a very long way in time.

The best known of the propliopithecids is called *Aegyptopithecus* (meaning "Egyptian ape"). *Aegyptopithecus* was about the size of a house cat, and in life would more closely have resembled some of the larger South American monkeys than any other primates living today. It probably came down from the trees only rarely, and it was a slow, careful climber that lived mostly on the abundant forest fruit.

Interestingly, *Aegyptopithecus* doesn't seem to have had a very much larger brain than a lemur. But unlike lemurs, males were bigger than females, and had bigger, almost daggerlike, canine teeth. This pattern fits with a complex social structure, with groups of numerous adult males and females, and the males competing for the females. And that's pretty typical for Old World higher primates as a whole. Lacking as it did any of the *specializations* of either the monkeys or the apes, *Aegyptopithecus* was probably about equally related to both.

CHAPTER SIX

TWO WORLDS OF MONKEYS

We've already seen that the term "monkey" doesn't mean that the New World and Old World primates known by that name are closely related. Each group is the result of a long independent evolutionary history. Nonetheless, each plays a broadly similar role in its own region.

NEW WORLD MONKEYS ▪ The monkeys of South and Central America are a very diverse group, with several dozen species. They are most abundant and most varied in the vast tropical forests of the Amazon River basin. Except for the species called night monkeys, all are active during the day. And like prosimians that are active by day, males and females often have different-colored coats.

All the New World primates are classified in the superfamily Ceboidea (named for *Cebus*, the organ-grinder's monkey). Scientists are still arguing about how this large group should be divided up. Traditionally, however, the smallest of them, the marmosets and tamarins, have been placed together because all their fingers and toes (except the big toes) are tipped with claws or, to be more exact, nails that have become modified to look like claws. Except for the tiny pygmy marmoset, which weighs about 4 ounces (113 grams), marmosets and tamarins typically weigh about 1 pound (0.5 kilogram) or a little less. They scurry around in the trees rather like squirrels, and they eat a variety of foods. Some of the marmosets specialize in gouging tree trunks and branches with their teeth to obtain nutritious gums, but all supplement their diets with insects and fruit. Tamarins eat mostly insects and fruit, adding buds and tender young leaves and once in a while a small vertebrate such as one of the tiny frog species that live in the forest canopy.

Marmosets most commonly live in pairs consisting of an adult male and female. Such pairs, with their offspring, may combine into larger groups that possibly make up "extended families" of related individuals.

The pygmy marmoset lives in the upper Amazon River basin.

Unusually among primates, marmosets tend to have twins or triplets rather than single young. Both parents cooperate in raising the young; indeed, the father may carry them around most of the time. Tamarins seem also to remain mostly with one mate, although they, too, come together into larger groups of up to nine or so animals. However, it seems that in some species, only one of the pairs within each larger group will produce young.

The larger South American primates are a varied lot. Among the smallest of them are the squirrel monkeys, which weigh no more than a pound or two. They eat mostly fruit, filling up with it early in the day before they undertake the more energetic task of searching for insects and spiders. They live in huge groups that may contain a hundred or more individuals. Not much bigger are the huge-eyed night monkeys. These primates live in family groups. Besides calling to each other they also communicate with smell, prosimian-style, using scent glands at the base of their tail.

There are too many kinds of South American monkeys to mention them all, but we must not forget the howler monkeys, the woolly and spider monkeys, and the capuchins. All of these have *prehensile* (grasping) tails that can be curled around branches to provide a "fifth limb," although the spider monkeys are better at doing this than the howlers or, especially, the capuchins. Howler monkeys are large, weighing up to 15 pounds (7 kilograms) or more, and eat mostly leaves. They live in groups of up to twenty individuals, with about twice as many adult females as males. They get their name from a specialized apparatus in the throat that amplifies their famous "roaring" calls.

Capuchins weigh up to about 8 pounds (3.6 kilograms), and live in groups ranging between about six and thirty individuals. They are very smart, and they have a wide variety of facial expressions. They prefer fruit, but they will eat a wide variety of forest products.

Spider monkeys are among the largest South American primates—up to 20 pounds (9 kilograms) or more—and include some of the most

The night monkey, or owl monkey, has enormous eyes.

Wooly spider
monkeys can
cling to
branches with
their long,
grasping tails.

appealing of all. With slender limbs and a long, prehensile tail that they use constantly as they move around in the forest canopy in search of fruit, they are astonishing acrobats. In their very flexible social system an individual may move around independently or join with others into groups that generally number up to twenty.

Finally, there are the sakis, medium-sized primates—around 5 pounds (2 kilograms)—that run and leap through the forest canopy with great agility. Fruits and seeds are their favorite food items, and they usually form small family groups.

Despite the great variety of South American primates, all live only in the forest. Unlike the Old World monkeys, this group seems never to have produced species that are adapted to life in more open country.

OLD WORLD MONKEYS ▪ The Old World monkeys are another highly successful group of primates. But apart from the invasion of open country by some species, they tend on the whole to be less varied than the monkeys of the New World. Perhaps this is because they have often had to share their habitat with apes, which were more widespread in the past than they are now. Whatever the case, while we recognize four or five major groups of monkeys in the New World, we recognize only two in the Old World.

Members of one of these groups, the *cercopithecines*, have been called "the hustlers of the primate order." They have spread to pretty much every tropical environment, as well as to some areas that get quite cold, and they eat just about anything that could possibly be eaten by a primate. The cercopithecines are found in both Africa and Asia, with a southern European outpost in Gibraltar, home of the Barbary macaques. All of them have cheek-pouches, big pockets in the walls of their mouths that they can stuff with vast amounts of food before going off to eat it in a safe place. Their favorite resting posture is a sitting position, and cercopithecines all have specialized pads on their bottoms that allow them to do this in comfort, wherever they are. The African cercopithecines include the guenons, vervets, baboons, and patas monkeys. They range in weight from about 10 to 70 pounds (4.5 to 32 kilograms). All are found south of the Sahara Desert, although the slender-limbed, fast-running patas monkeys survive on the desert's inhospitable fringes.

The Asian cercopithecines are all various species of macaques, which are perhaps the greatest opportunists of all. They are found all the way from western India to Japan, and from cold northern China and the snowy slopes of the Himalayas to the steamy jungles of Indonesia. They also live in parts of northern Africa, where there are no other cercopithecines.

Cercopithecines can be found in all environments, from rainforest to dry, open tree savanna. They are famous for their intelligence, especially in the way they deal with each other. Most live in rather large groups (the range is from about a dozen to a hundred or more), with many individuals of all ages. Within these groups, very complex relationships develop among individuals. Status is very important within large groups, and sometimes high social rank is achieved by forming alliances as well as by confronting rivals.

Cercopithecine behavior is flexible in other ways as well. For example, savanna-living vervets normally take shelter in trees from dogs or other ground-dwelling attackers. There they utter loud cries to warn others of the danger. But if they are on a farm when they spot a dog, they stay quiet and melt away into hiding. In such places dogs are often accompanied by armed farmers, and attracting attention might attract bullets, too!

Vervets are a very good example of a cercopithecine species that has adapted well to human interference with its environment. While they can't compete with more specialized forest monkeys in the natural forest habitat, they thrive in areas disrupted by farmers. They prefer to eat fruit and insects, but they will readily eat flowers and leaves and pretty much anything else as well. In one instance, when invading rats ate up their usual food supply, the vervets adjusted by eating the rats!

Right: The macaque has cheek-pouches for carrying away food that it finds. Below: Like other cercopithecines, baboons live in groups and develop complex relationships.

The other major group of Old World monkeys is the *colobine leaf monkeys*. Most species live in dense forests, although these include forests of many different kinds. Leaves are their main food source, and although you might think that a forest is full of leaves, and is thus a well-stocked larder for them, it's not quite as simple as that. Trees don't like having their leaves eaten, and one way they discourage this from happening is by pumping them full of poisonous chemicals. Animals that eat lots of leaves thus need special ways of eliminating the poisons they take in with their food.

Leaves are also full of tough cellulose. This is difficult to digest, and so leaf-eaters also need elaborate digestive systems. Individual leaves are also not very nutritious, so leaf-eaters need to eat lots of them. Putting all this together means that leaf-eaters need to spend large amounts of time eating and digesting and *detoxifying* their food. This is why colobines are in general less active in other ways than are the cercopithecines.

The best known of the leaf monkeys are the many kinds of colobus monkeys in Africa, and the langurs in Asia. Different kinds of colobus monkeys prefer different kinds of leaves, and social systems differ too. Some live in smallish groups of about eight to fifteen, with only one dominant male. Young males are driven out of the group when they mature and have to roam around on their own until they can take over another group. Other colobus monkeys live in groups that have several adult males, and it is the females that move from one group to another. Males, which mostly weigh in at about 20 to 30 pounds (9 to 14 kilograms), are much bigger than females, which range from 15 to 20 pounds (7 to 9 kilograms).

The langurs include one widespread and very adaptable species that is quite at home on the ground, and is often found in areas of open woodland and in farming areas where its members frequently raid crops. These are the Hanuman langurs. Revered in Hindu mythology, Hanuman langurs are often seen in Hindu temples, where they are fed by believers. Weighing

Above: Adaptable vervets often live near farms. Right: The black colobus monkey prefers a specialized diet of leaves.

**The male proboscis monkey
has an unforgettable nose.**

about 40 pounds (18 kilograms), Hanuman males are about half again as big as females, and compete strenuously for mates. These monkeys live in groups that may number as many as sixty individuals, but more typically average about twenty. The core of the group is made up of adult females and their offspring, with a variable number of males joining them.

Most other Asian colobines, including other langur species, follow a leaf-eating life in the forests. Among these are the remarkable-looking proboscis monkeys. The large adult males—twice the size of females, up to 50 pounds (23 kilograms)—develop huge, bulbous noses. These monkeys live in parts of Borneo, a huge island off the coast of Southeast Asia. They are found mostly in coastal swamp and river-edge forests. Often these forests are dominated by mangrove trees, whose leaves provide an unusual diet for a primate. Also unusually for a primate, proboscis monkeys will readily dive into the water and swim away to evade an attacker. They live in groups of from ten to sixty individuals, with adults of both sexes, and individuals seem to transfer readily between neighboring groups.

Even though some species are very specialized, the Asian colobines are in general very *adaptable*, and able to exist in a huge range of habitats. It is certainly their remarkable ability to adapt to different circumstances that explains the success of both major groups of Old World monkeys. It may also explain why the apes have been steadily losing ground to them over the past 15 million years or so.

CHAPTER SEVEN

THE RISE AND FALL
OF THE APES

With the beginning of the Miocene epoch, which lasted from about 24 to 5 million years ago, we begin to pick up fossil evidence for the evolution of the monkeys and of Hominoidea, the group to which we and the apes belong. The first Old World monkey fossil crops up as early as about 23 million years ago, and by about 19 million years ago fossils show that both the colobines and cercopithecines existed.

The early Old World monkey fossil record is quite limited, though, and most of what we know about anthropoid evolution at this early time concerns our group, the *hominoids*. Fossils have come to light largely as a result of a series of geological events that began in eastern Africa early in the Miocene.

This series of events was linked to the creation of the East African Rift Valley, a great scar that runs down through the middle of Africa from the Red Sea in the north to Mozambique in the south. (The formation of this huge valley is, in fact, the first stage in a process that, millions of years from now, may divide Africa into two continental masses, as the valley gets wider and deeper and the sea flows into it.)

For people interested in primate evolution, the great feature of the Rift Valley is that in the early stages of its formation the center of Africa was lifted up along its length. This process involved lots of geological activity in the regions of East Africa that we now know as Kenya and Uganda. It led to the laying down of rocks in which a great variety of early hominoid fossils have been found.

EARLY HOMINOIDS ▪ These early hominoids were the forerunners of both the apes and humans, but it is important to remember that they were neither one nor the other. They were primitive species, equally distant from both humans and apes. They were certainly not monkeys, although in contrast to their descendants they did have arms and legs that were proportioned rather like those of monkeys today. The best known of these early hominoids was called *Proconsul*.

Several species of *Proconsul* are known, and a bounty of fossils discovered on an island in Lake Victoria show that it was a rather generalized tree-dweller. It was quite heavily built and rather slow moving and, like today's hominoids, it lacked a tail. However, the bones of *Proconsul* show none of the features that modern apes have acquired for suspending the body in the trees. Similarly, *Proconsul* lacked the special modifications of the hand that great apes have for moving around on the ground.

Instead, *Proconsul* retained an ancestral Old World primate body shape. This kind of anatomy seems to have been suited to foraging for fruit in moist tropical forest habitats. The other fossil species found alongside *Proconsul* are typical of forest environments, and *Proconsul*'s teeth look like those of a fruit-eater rather than a leaf-eater. Some scientists think that the features seen in monkey fossils of similar age indicate, in contrast, that the ancestral Old World monkeys had moved out into more open country.

Anatomical details—for example, the shape of the molar teeth—show that *Proconsul* and many of its early Miocene relatives stand close to the ancestry of all of the living hominoids, the gibbons of Asia as well as the great apes and ourselves.

Beginning about 17 million years ago, we start to find fossil evidence in Arabia and Africa for more advanced hominoids. Among other features, these new hominoids had very thick enamel on their chewing teeth. They seem to have lived in more open woodland habitats than the more primitive forms. Such habitats would have produced food more seasonally than tropical forests do. So it's possible that the hominoids with thick-enameled teeth had broadened their diet by cracking harder items like nuts, something for which this new adaptation would have been very useful. But we cannot identify among them a species that is clearly ancestral to any living ape.

By about 13 million years ago, fossils of more advanced hominoids begin to be found outside Africa. These include a European form known as *Dryopithecus*. However, most scientists don't think that this hominoid and its relatives were ancestral to any of today's apes. It still seems most likely that the earliest ancestor of apes and humans lived in Africa.

Nonetheless, the first really convincing fossil evidence that we have for an ancestor of any living ape comes from a hominoid called *Sivapithecus*, which lived outside Africa. This primate had thick-enameled chewing teeth, and its fossils have been found at sites in Greece, Turkey, India, and Pakistan that are dated to between 7 and 11 million years ago. The best specimens of *Sivapithecus* come from Pakistan, and they paint a very interesting picture.

Sivapithecus had a face that resembles that of the modern orangutan quite closely. This is significant, because orangutans have a very unusual skull. The eye sockets are tall and narrow, and the lower face projects out considerably below the nose. There can be little doubt that *Sivapithecus* lies somewhere in the ancestry of the orangutan. However, it retained the more generalized monkeylike skeleton of the primitive hominoids. This kind of example shows that ancestors do not evolve smoothly and gradually into their descendants. Instead, new characteristics may be acquired at different times.

***Proconsul*, a forerunner of modern apes, was a tree-dweller.**

We are still looking for convincing ancestors of the other great apes, but so far with no luck, although it is suggested from time to time that one fossil form or another does resemble an African ape. One problem is that we don't know of many fossil sites that represent the kinds of habitats in which ancestral apes lived. But where we do have sites it's pretty plain that, as time passed, there were fewer and fewer different kinds of hominoids. Apparently, as world environments slowly became cooler and drier, forests became smaller and woodlands and grasslands spread, favoring the more adaptable monkeys over the apes.

The known fossil record suggests that in the Miocene there were many more hominoid species than monkey species. Today monkeys are abundant, while only a handful of ape species survive in a very few areas. As competitors for habitat, monkeys seem to have been vastly more successful than apes—with one exception: ourselves. Strangely, we may owe our own origins to the same changes in climate that gave the monkeys their chance. But that's a story for later on. Now, let's look at the modern apes—our own closest relatives.

CHAPTER EIGHT

ASIAN ACROBATS

Even though they are few in number, the species of living hominoids (the gibbons, the orangutans, the chimpanzees, the gorillas, and humans) make up a rather oddly assorted group. What do we all have in common?

First of all, today's hominoids all share in the greatest degree the primate trends we looked at earlier. We all depend almost exclusively on vision rather than smell. We all share at least a strong tendency toward upright body posture, with a broad, shallow chest (in contrast to the narrow, deep chest of the four-footed monkeys). We all have arms that move very freely in all directions. We have small numbers of offspring, with the longest growing-up (and therefore learning) periods. We live the longest. And we have the largest and most complex brains. We also have a lot of less obvious features in common (such as the shape of our teeth). It is clear that for all our variety, we hominoids are one another's closest relatives.

GIBBONS ▪ Let's begin to look at our hominoid group in more detail. The "lesser apes," the gibbons, are the smallest of the living hominoids and the most distantly related to us. The gibbons occupy only a rather small area of the world, in Southeast Asia and part of the enormous Indonesian island chain. Despite this limited range, there are more species of them than of any other hominoid.

Gibbons are most remarkable for the way they move around in the trees. They have very long arms, which they use to suspend themselves beneath branches in the forest. When they are traveling through the trees they swing from one branch to the next with extraordinary speed and agility. When on the ground (and also on the tops of large branches) they prefer to walk on two legs, holding the body upright. This posture keeps their long arms out of the way as they progress. When feeding, they use their ability to suspend themselves to move even into the outermost parts of the trees, holding bunches of fine twigs in their long, powerful hands.

The gibbon's long arms allow it to swing gracefully from one tree limb to the next.

Adult male and female gibbons seem to mate for life, and the young remain in the family group until they are mature, which usually means for seven years or more. A single infant is born every two or three years, and spends its first year under the constant care of its mother. Among the biggest kind of gibbons, called siamangs, the father takes over after this, but among the smaller gibbons species the mother continues to watch over the young carefully for several years. During this long period of growing up the young gibbons learn a great deal about the world in which they live and about how to behave toward other members of their species.

Gibbons live in quite small territories which they defend against their neighbors. One of their main ways of announcing their claim to a territory is by loud calls, in which both adults join. This "duetting" is a familiar sound of the forest, and an experienced listener can tell which pair is calling by the pattern of the song. When gibbon groups meet at the boundaries of their home ranges, males perform elaborate defense rituals, chasing each other around while the females "cheer them on" with loud calls.

As seems typical for species where males and females pair for life, and adult males thus don't compete with one another for females, the two sexes are of pretty much the same size. Most gibbons weigh about 11 to 15 pounds (5 to 7 kilograms); siamangs may get up to 25 pounds (11 kilograms). Both sexes also sport quite large and daggerlike canine teeth of similar size. Among other apes, males have larger canines than females do.

Most gibbons feed chiefly on fruit (they especially love figs, of several wild species), and siamangs supplement their diet with quite a few leaves. Some species eat flowers and insects. But there are quite a few species that we know nothing about, and it is possible that we may in the end be left with little knowledge of them. The tall forests that are their home are being destroyed by humans at an amazing rate, and many populations may disappear before scientists have a chance to study them. For all that, though, as a group gibbons are less immediately endangered than their larger ape relatives.

CHAPTER NINE

THE GREAT APES

There are only three main kinds of great apes living today. These are the gorillas, chimpanzees, and orangutans. We belong among them, but scientists are uncertain which of the great apes is our closest relative. However, if a vote were to be held on this question right now, it's probable that the chimpanzees would win. Like gibbons and humans, all great apes lack tails, and next to us they have the largest brains and longest lifespans of any primates.

ORANGUTANS ▪ The only great apes found outside Africa are the orangutans, whose name means "man of the forest" in the Malay language. Bearing splendid coats of long, shaggy red hair, they are nowadays confined to tropical forests in the two biggest islands of Indonesia, Sumatra and Borneo. Not so long ago, however, they were more widespread, with populations on the Asian mainland as well.

Male orangs grow very big, up to 200 pounds (91 kilograms) or more, while females are only about half that size. Females and young are thus rather more acrobatic in the trees than are the males, which spend more time on the ground. Males and females alike move around in the branches

**Orangutan mothers and babies
form strong bonds.**

in a very deliberate way; they suspend themselves by as many limbs as possible, using their long, hooked hands and feet. On the ground, they curl their hands into fists, bearing their weight on the middle knuckles.

Females and males for the most part live separate lives, though sometimes several individuals will travel through the forest together for some time. Also, matings often occur after a male and a female have kept company for a week or two. But by far the strongest social bond is between mothers and their young. Births are quite rare, though, occurring as much as five years apart. Female orangutans grow up faster than males do, becoming mature at around the age of eight. Males may take almost twice as long. As a male orangutan matures, he develops large fatty "flanges" around his face, making his head look even bigger than it is.

An orangutan's daily round consists mostly of visits to trees bearing ripe fruit—like gibbons, orangs especially favor figs. Often several orangs will meet at a fruiting tree. They usually ignore one another, though sometimes the arrival of a particularly large male may scare the others away.

Most scientists, though not all, think that orangutans are the least closely related to us of all the great apes. But any zookeeper will tell you that in captivity orangutans are the most ingenious ape of all. They are especially good at picking locks!

GORILLAS ▪ Gorillas are found today only in a couple of parts of western and central Africa. The largest of all the hominoids, male gorillas may weigh in at over 400 pounds (182 kilograms) in the wild, and one bored and overweight captive gorilla achieved 772 pounds (347 kilograms)! Females weigh in at a trimmer 200 pounds (91 kilograms) or so.

Gorilla groups are smallish, containing from two to about twenty individuals. They are led by a dominant male, usually known as a "silverback" because of the whitish fur that develops across the shoulders when

This gorilla family group includes a big silverback male, a female, and youngsters of various ages.

males mature at about twelve years of age. When they mature, males don't immediately leave the group they were born in, though most eventually will. Males tolerate infants and sometimes play with them, but the burden of child rearing is on the mothers.

These apes roam around in home ranges that may be as large as several square miles, and because of their large size they spend a lot of time on the ground. When they're on the ground, they curl their fists more tightly than orangs, bearing their weight on the first knuckles of each hand. Chimpanzees do this, too. Gorillas construct nests of leaves, branches, and other vegetation to sleep in. Especially in the case of the heavier males, these are often on the ground.

Despite their fearsome reputation, gorillas live a pretty peaceable existence (though males occasionally battle for group leadership). They spend most of their waking time foraging for plants to eat. Gorillas especially like leaves, shoots, and stems, though they also eat fruit and flowers and occasionally insects.

CHIMPANZEES ▪ Chimpanzees come in two kinds: the "common" chimpanzees of western and central Africa, and the "pygmy" chimpanzees (better called bonobos), which live in the forests of the Congo basin. Despite their name, bonobos actually are hardly any smaller than regular chimpanzees. However, bonobos spend almost all of their time in the treetops, perhaps because they live in denser forests. Common chimpanzees spend more time on the ground. In both kinds of chimpanzee, males are only a little bigger than females, the average male common chimpanzee weighing about 100 pounds (45 kilograms) to the female's 90 pounds (40 kilograms).

Common chimpanzees are amazingly adaptable, occupying habitats that range from rain forest to quite dry open woodland. The best-studied chimpanzees are at Gombe Stream in Tanzania, in East Africa, where the environment is quite open. Here social patterns are very changeable, and new surprises (such as "warfare"—members of one band deliberately killing members of another) are being discovered all the time.

The Gombe chimpanzees eat mostly fruit, but they also go for animal foods. For example, they occasionally gang up to hunt monkeys or other small mammals, and they gladly devour any birds' eggs they come across. Most famously, however, they go "fishing" for termites. To do this, they find an active termite mound, and then strip the leaves off a twig. They then push the spindly twig into a hole on the mound, where it will be

A mother chimp "fishes" for termites as her baby looks on.

attacked by termites. When they withdraw the twig, the termites clinging to it can be eagerly licked off and eaten. Females seem to indulge in termiting more than males do. Hunting is a male activity, though males share some of the food with females and young.

The Gombe chimpanzees live in well-defined communities that appear to split up when numbers become too large (about eighty). Members of these communities, both male and female, may spend a good bit of time foraging alone, but within the community they often combine into groups of varying sizes. Males seem to associate with each other more than with females, whose strongest bond is with their offspring. Males may form bands to patrol the edges of their home ranges, and they sometimes attack lone animals belonging to neighboring communities.

Bonobo communities seem to be a little smaller—perhaps fifty individuals or so—but these primates are usually seen out foraging in groups of about four or five. Males seem to associate with females more than is typical of common chimpanzees.

Stripping twigs for termiting is clearly a primitive form of tool making, an activity that was for long thought to be uniquely human. But experimental studies have shown that even with training chimpanzees don't develop the same understanding of how stone breaks that the earliest human tool makers had.

Attempts to teach chimpanzees sign language have, on the other hand, shown that chimpanzees can acquire quite a good vocabulary of signs, as gorillas also have managed to do. But what this actually tells us about the evolution of human communication is not quite clear. Behaviorally, humans are quite different from even their closest living relatives, and now we'll look briefly at how we became so different.

CHAPTER TEN

THE SAME BUT DIFFERENT

When we compare ourselves with our closest living relatives, the apes, it's quite easy to see how different we are. We walk upright, leaving our hands free to make things and carry them around; we have big brains and an unmatched intelligence and flexibility of behavior. Our last common ancestor with the apes probably lived well under 10 million years ago, so we've obviously come a long way in what is quite a short time in the history of evolution. How did we do it?

The earliest fossils known of a specifically human ancestor belong to a species called *Australopithecus afarensis* that lived in Africa between about 3 and 4 million years ago. The best known representative of this species is "Lucy," the skeleton of a young female who lived about 3.2 million years ago. Lucy and her kind were upright walkers who lived on the edges of forests and out in the open savannas, but there's not much else about them that you could call human. They were small, with a big face and a small brain, rather like apes; they didn't make stone tools; and even their upright bodies had different proportions from ours, with rather long arms and short legs.

Right up until about 2 or 2.5 million years ago all of our ancestors and fossil relatives were not much different from Lucy. Then some of them

Fossil skulls provide evidence of early humans.

started to make stone tools, which they used to cut up animal carcasses they found, but physically they hadn't changed much.

The first really big physical change came at about 1.8 million years ago, when tall humans with modern bodies appeared on the scene. These early humans had brains that were a bit bigger than Lucy's, but not nearly as large as ours. And at first, they didn't make tools that were any more sophisticated than the stone chips of the first toolmakers. Pretty soon, though, stone tools were invented that were purposely made to a particular shape, most notably the large, teardrop-shaped hand ax.

The hand ax seems to be a good general-purpose tool for butchering dead animals, but most archaeologists don't think that the first hand–ax makers actually hunted the animals they cut up; probably they found them after lions and other carnivores had killed them. It's likely that they got most of their food the way Lucy had, by gathering plant foods they found on the savanna.

As time passed, bigger-brained human species came on the scene, and they found more efficient ways of making stone tools. And at some time earlier (perhaps a lot earlier) than about 1 million years ago, some humans finally exited from Africa, moving into cooler environments to the north. But still there was no major revolution in lifestyle. The Neanderthals, early humans who lived in Europe and western Asia beginning about 200,000 years ago, had brains as big as ours, and made beautifully crafted stone tools. But even they were not as sophisticated hunters as we are.

Great changes finally came with people who looked just like us. Such people probably arose in Africa at some time over about 100,000 years ago, but even then we don't pick up evidence of a major change in behavior until about 40,000 years ago. Then, for unknown reasons, these people started behaving in a way more familiar to us. They made tools from bone and antler as well as from stone (and maybe wood). When they entered Europe and Australia they brought with them art and symbolism and music. They were excellent hunters even of the biggest game, and those who first came to Australia must have been excellent navigators, too, for they had to cross many miles of open ocean.

The early humans who first ventured out into the savannas 4 or 5 million years ago were certainly doing things no primate had ever done before. But it seems clear that the real behavioral leap, the one that made us different in the ways that make us particularly special, only came very late indeed. We are primates, and we always will be. But, very recently in our evolutionary history, something happened—something that we don't yet understand—that made us truly different. And that something is the true mystery of human evolution.

AFTERWORD

As we've seen, we humans represent the high point (so far) of many of the trends that have been used to distinguish primates as a group. But just as we can't look at ourselves as the top primate in a series that gradually leads to us, we can't think of ourselves as a result that *had* to happen through a process of evolutionary improvement over millions of years. Evolution just doesn't work that way. It simply grasps opportunities that arise. If anything different had happened in the past, our ancestors' descendants today would be very different from us. Our evolution consists of a unique series of events, and if we were to go back to that ancestral Paleocene primate and start over, it would be very unlikely indeed that in another 65 million years another species exactly like ourselves would stride the earth.

We're here, though, and we're something truly unusual. So unusual, in fact, that we control nature well enough to be a real threat to it. Humans have a unique ability to destroy the environment, as well as to enjoy it. And as human populations expand all over the world, habitats are disappearing forever. Many of the habitats that are vanishing most quickly are the only homes of our own primate relatives. And if we don't take immediate steps to stop this destruction of habitats, we humans will soon be the lone primate in a world that is increasingly unappealing to live in.

GLOSSARY

Adaptable. Able to accommodate to a wide variety of environmental conditions.

Anthropoids. The "higher" primates: monkeys, apes, humans, and various extinct families.

Cercopithecines. One of the two subfamilies of Old World monkeys, possessing cheek pouches and specialized sitting pads.

Colobines. The other subfamily of Old World monkeys, often referred to as the "leaf monkeys."

Detoxification. The removal of poisons from food in the digestive tract.

Diurnal. Active during daylight.

Diversity. The variety of species.

Evolution. The process through which new kinds of living things arise in nature.

Extinction. The dying out of species.

Fossils. Any evidence of past life. Among primates, most often the petrified bones and teeth of dead individuals.

Genes. Parts of the DNA molecule that carry out specific functions in the building of each new individual.

Habitat. The environment in which an animal population lives.

Hominoids. The superfamily of higher primates which includes the greater and lesser apes and humans.

Leaf monkeys. The colobines of the Old World, many species of which have specialized diets of leaves.

Nocturnal. Active at night.

Nucleic acids. The class of molecules that includes DNA, the molecule that contains the genetic instructions from which each new individual is built.

Parapithecids. Members of an extinct family of early anthropoids.

Predator. An animal that kills and feeds on other animals.

Prehensile tail. A tail capable of "grasping" by curling at the end.

Propliopithecids. Members of an extinct family of early anthropoids probably related to both the Old and New World "higher" primates.

Prosimians. The "lower" primates: the lemurs, lorises, bushbabies, and tarsiers.

Specializations. Characteristics that depart from the ancestral condition and that are usually related to a specific way of life.

Vertebrates. Animals with backbones.

FURTHER READING

Elwood, Anne. *Zoobooks: Chimps and Bonobos*. San Diego: Wildlife Education Inc., 1990.

Fleagle, John. *Primate Adaptation and Evolution*. New York: Academic Press, 1988.

Jolly, Alison. *A World Like Our Own*. New Haven: Yale University Press, 1980.

Kavanagh, Michael. *A Complete Guide to Monkeys, Apes and Other Primates*. London: Jonathan Cape, 1983.

Kogod, Charles (editor). *The Great Apes: Between Two Worlds*. Washington, DC: National Geographic Society, 1993.

Lemmon, Tess, and John Butler. *Apes*. New York: Tickner and Fields, 1993.

Napier, Prue. *Monkeys and Apes*. New York: Grosset & Dunlap, 1972.

Peterson, Dale. *The Deluge and the Ark: A Journey Into Primate Worlds*. New York: Avon Books, 1989.

Wexo, John Bennett. *Zoobooks: The Apes*. San Diego: Wildlife Education, Inc., 1986.

Wexo, John Bennett. *Zoobooks: Gorillas*. San Diego: Wildlife Education, Inc., 1991.

INDEX

ABOUT THE AUTHOR

*Ian Tattersall is chairman of the department
of anthropology at the American Museum of
Natural History in New York City and is curator
of that museum's Hall of Human Biology and
Evolution, which opened in 1993.*

*He holds a doctorate from Yale University,
has taught and lectured widely, and acts as a
consultant for a wide range of organizations,
including the World Bank, the World Wildlife
Fund, and broadcast and print media.*

*Dr. Tattersall has done field work at sites
all over the world, including Madagascar,
Borneo, northern and southern Africa, and
South America. His work in human and nonhuman
primate evolution, primate ecology and behavior,
and related fields has brought him widespread
recognition and numerous grants and awards.*